Uber Diva

Hot Tips for Drivers and Passengers of Uber and Lyft

Charles St. Anthony

Impossibly Glamorous Studios
San Francisco

Copyright 2017
Published by Impossibly Glamorous Studios
ISBN-13: 978-0-9983185-6-1
First Edition

Edited by Marcella Hammer
Cover Illustration of "Simone" designed by Charles St. Anthony and illustrated by Toonimals. Interior illustrations also by Toonimals.
Disclaimers:

Names, details and locations have been changed to protect the anonymity of people in these pages. This memoir involves actual people I have met and experiences I have lived through. As a work of creative nonfiction, in some cases, accounts have been paraphrased or embellished for purposes of parody or comic effect. However, I have done my best to maintain accuracy in the numbers and figures in the infographic.

The views, information, or opinions expressed the opinion of the author who worked as a private contractor for Uber and Lyft. The observations stated herein are solely the author's personal opinions and do not necessarily represent those of Uber, Lyft, Apple, Google or Twitter.

This work is protected under the copyright Fair Use Act for *de minimis* use of copyright protected material for review, commentary, education, criticism and parody.

The author assumes no responsibility or liability for any errors or omissions in the content of this work. The information contained is provided on an "as is" basis with no guarantees of completeness, accuracy, usefulness or timeliness.

Cover illustration of Simone (the diva) is purely an image from Charles St. Anthony's imagination and not based on any other person—living or deceased.

The Contents

Crashing to a Halt 6

About That Coin 12

Pre-Game Necessities 15

Highway to the Danger Zone 22

The Petty Olympics 25

One in the Pink 35

By the Numbers 39

Sideshow Freaks 43

Tell Me Sweet Little Lies 51

Glitch Nation 55

Rode Hard and Put Away Wet 58

Random Ass Things I Laughed About to Keep Myself Entertained While Driving 61

My Acknowledgements 63

About the Author 65

Crashing to a Halt

2:00 a.m. on a Thursday morning, I pull up to a house. Lights flicker on the second floor, and I assume some college students are partying upstairs. Just a few more rides, and I'll hit my target. By driving a total of twenty-five rides, Uber will give me a $70 bonus. I turn my hazard lights on and fiddle with my mobile phone.

Trust me. This diva never thought life would turn out this way.

A contract I had at a major tech company ended sooner than I had anticipated leaving me in a bind. I had begrudgingly moved from my spunky San Francisco neighborhood to the suburban doldrums of Silicon Valley to be closer to their headquarters. It was only a contract job, and after a mere ten months, they disposed of me like a used up paper plate at a pot luck dinner. I ruminate on this misfortune while waiting for my passenger to join me.

I feel intense pain and am disoriented. *I'm going to die. I'm going to die.* I don't know what's happening, but I struggle to open my car door. I can't breathe. My whole body reverberates with a metallic vibration. I try to walk but fall on the ground as people from inside the house come out to see what's going on.

"Are you OK?" a young man asks.

"Call 911! Call 911!" I tell him as I attempt to gather my senses. Later I realize the impact had knocked me unconscious. My car spun completely around and smacked a parked car next to me, but I don't remember spinning about like the Disneyland teacups.

"The guy who hit you is over there," a young man says. Despite nearly dying a couple moments earlier, I feel like I downed a couple Mountain Dews. I start to walk around energetically as my body fills with what I later realize is adrenaline.

About 100 yards down Hedding Street, the car that hit me sits in disarray. I pull out my phone to get photos. *You can't trust people these days. Better take photos as evidence.* I think as I walk toward a shadowy figure on this residential street.

The first man I encounter is a slim Asian guy. He agrees to let me video record his account. Considering the other driver had hit a parked car with its hazard lights blinking on an empty street, I figure he must be intoxicated.

"Did you smell alcohol on him?"

"I'm just a bystander."

"But you smelled alcohol on him, yes?"

"Yes."

I approach the other car which has been rendered immobile from the incident.

"Are you OK? I'm going to take some pictures."

He nodded.

"Can I have a look at your ID?" I say as I photograph his license plate.

He hands me his wallet, and I take a blurry photo of his ID. The permit says he is from a town I've never heard of in Mexico. "Do you mind if I film you?"

He weeps, but says I can video record him, "I can still run if you want," he pleads in the video. Even though I'm in pain and my car is totaled, I feel pity for him. His face contorts as he realizes the enormity of his fuck up.

"Have you been drinking tonight?"

"Yes. Yes."

I feel dizzy and disoriented, so the police recommend I pay a visit to the ER. The Mexican guy who hit me runs off on foot. I don't realize that, because I'm on my way to the hospital. I take a couple photos to post on social media so my friends would know I am OK. After posting them I delete them quickly. *Who posts to Instagram from an ambulance? God, I look like such an asshole.*

A ride from where the accident happened on East Hedding Street in San Jose to El Camino Hospital in Mountain View costs approximately $16 on Uber at time of writing. The bill which I would receive from Rural Metro Ambulance Company a couple weeks later was $2381.50.

That's on top of the other bills from the ER visit that included bills from El Camino Hospital ($3578.05), X-rays ($297), El Camino Pathology Med Group ($381.25) and California Emergency Physicians ($480). After a couple hours at the ER, the physicians deemed it OK to go home, but not before accruing more than $8000 in bills from a solitary ER visit. Due to the intense back pain I experienced in the following weeks, I would have more bills on the way. All from a night I was hoping to hit my $75 bonus from Uber. A cost benefit analysis would say this endeavor as a rideshare driver was a horrible return on investment.

My story is sort of a worst case scenario. Well, not the worst case. I survived. I've felt back pain for months, but at least I wasn't disfigured or maimed. However, the accident flipped my life upside down.

Rideshare services such as Uber are an increasingly popular way to make extra money. Should you do it? Is it for you? I write this essay for a reader who might be wanting to make some extra scratch via Uber or Lyft, so you can make an informed decision as to whether it is for you. I also include some juicy factoids for passengers as well. When this diva puts out, she really puts out. If you join Uber or Lyft, you might be able to pay off that student loan faster. Or maybe save money for a down payment on that house you want. Or you could end up like me, carless and jobless after a drunk driver destroyed my main source of income.

About That Coin

Do you have enough money? Aside from the wealthy who have tapped into enough resources that their days can be spent in leisure, most of us are burdened with this human concept of money. We devote the majority of our time in the acquisition of it. We must prostitute our minds and bodies doing activities that we would rather not in order to have "stuff." The economics of daily life is especially annoying nowadays, since long gone are the days when a car, house and family livelihood could be harnessed by one adult male's salary. Dual incomes and multiple money streams have become the norm. If you want even a mediocre existence in a desirable location, when you are not working you still need to be working.

The gig economy has allowed technology to create even more work by having supply meet demand for a growing cadre of activities. Need someone to walk your dog? An app called Wag! has you covered. Don't feel like assembling that IKEA bed? Task Rabbit can connect you to people willing to do chores on demand. And of course when you need a car, you can book Uber or its equivalent in most major cities across the globe.

I first considered Uber due to the exorbitant nature of prices in the Bay Area. I worked full-time as a contractor for big tech companies such as Google and Twitter, but had yet to network my way into a permanent position. The type of work I was doing was called "content review," which is a catch-all term for people who examine apps, social media posts and other public content hosted by one of these companies.

You needed to be thick-skinned as a lot of these jobs involved looking at porn and gore. Google Play and Apple iTunes do not support pornography, but that doesn't stop developers from trying to sneak questionable content into their products. Just call me the titty whisperer. If there is an errant nipple or wayward vagina displaying on your computer screen, I am certain I can find it. Twitter, however, is a booby extravaganza. You are welcome to post as many cunts, cocks and mammaries as you like on Twitter. The images must be of people who are of legal age, consensually photographed and not appear in your profile avatar or background header. Anyway, these contracts were proving to be a dead end for me career-wise, so I decided that ridesharing might be a good way to get ahead financially while I worked my day jobs. Also, as I had written about driving a taxi in my hilarious mini-memoir *San Francisco Daddy*, I knew that as a comedy writer doing rideshare would contain a mother lode of good material.

This side hustle became my main hustle, though. Once my contract ended sooner than expected, my sole income became ridesharing. Since I was living in Silicon Valley—the white hot epicenter of the tech zeitgeist—I knew that this would be a great way to find funny stories to write about. That's how much I love you dear reader. I love you enough to ferry around entitled Silicon Valley twats in my party Corolla for six months.

Pre-Game Necessities

Every job has its equipment. A doctor needs a stethoscope and thermometers. A stripper needs a few choice G-strings and a pole. In the same way, you should stock up on the essentials for your job before hitting the road.

First, get all the insurance. Become the Svengali of insurance. Get so much insurance, it is spewing out of your wazoo.

Specifically, get something called a "rideshare endorsement" as that will cover you in the event of an accident. If your regular car insurance finds out you have been driving for Uber or Lyft without the rideshare endorsement, you might not get anything in the case of an accident like mine. Once you start driving for Lyft and Uber, you are now appropriating your vehicle for commercial purposes, so make sure you have the insurance that applies to how you use your car.

I found myself extremely grateful that I had this type of insurance from State Farm. When the insurance adjuster deemed my Toyota a total loss, they paid out $14,680 dollars (the cash value of my car) and $1321 in taxes. Alas, before my accident I did not realize that medical was not covered by the type of plan I selected from State Farm, so I am still waiting to hear whether my health insurance will pay the close to $10,000 in hospital and chiropractic bills I have accrued.

Once the insurance question is settled, you will need a few small items that riders will expect you to have, and if you don't have them you might get stars deducted in your rating.

- Phone mount – I personally found the vent mount most effective, since they seemed stable. I suggest you look at online reviews on YouTube and other places to find which one will be safest and most comfortable for you to use. Nothing looks more unprofessional (or dangerous) than a rideshare driver holding their phone in their hands while driving.

- FasTrak/E-ZPass – Most major metro areas have toll roads and bridges you'll need to cross in order to get your passengers around. In the Bay Area, they have something called a FasTrak you can usually purchase from a drug store. You then add your credit card information online so you can zoom through the toll charges without stopping. You don't want to be fishing in your pocket for a few quarters when you have a passenger that is in a hurry to get to the airport.

- Bluetooth earpiece – Sometimes you need to call passengers when you are searching for their home, and a Bluetooth earpiece is useful since you'll want to be hands-free.

- Bottled water – I advise picking up small bottles of water from Costco or Target to give out to passengers. I found that people did not want a particularly large bottle of water for their trips. A small 10 – 12 fluid ounce (296 – 355 ml) sippy bottle of water will suffice. For example, the 12 fluid ounce Aquafina bottles at Wal-Mart are perfect. Having free amenities such as this will raise your star rating.

- Air freshener – I experimented with several air fresheners, and I found Febreze "Bora Bora" to receive the most positive response from my passengers.

- Gasoline price app – The one type of overhead that you will not be able to escape most likely is gasoline. I made use of an app called Gas Buddy daily to find the most reasonable gasoline prices in my vicinity.

- Wiper for rain – The Corolla I leased had a serious drawback in that often rain would accumulate on the back window and make it difficult to see. If you have no rear window wiper, I would suggest purchasing something to wipe excess rain off for the safety of you and your passenger.

- Candy – Many drivers give out candy when they first begin driving, and I believe it is a good way to drive up your star rating. Halloween-sized Twix got me the best ratings, while Tootsie Pops got the worst. Bite-sized Snickers landed somewhere in the middle. Eventually, I stopped providing candy, since people are assholes and will litter the wrappers on the floor like they are at a movie theater (even when I provided a small garbage receptacle in the back seat).

- Auxiliary Cord – Having an aux cord and letting your passenger play DJ can be a good way to raise your rating. Who doesn't love to pump their favorite bop on the way to a party? Having said that, "Hell is other people's music." For example, "Bad and Boujee" by rap trio Migos held the top spot on the Billboard Hot 100 and played constantly on the radio during a large portion of my tenure as a driver. But if I hear about that fucking crock pot one more time, this diva's ears might start bleeding.

For every track you feel is a total banger, fifteen other people will find your taste to be intensely annoying. Also, dicking around with the sound system while you are driving is a good way to get into an accident. I always found the '80s FM station to be a safe choice as most people like the '80s. Young people might want something more current, though. Further, passengers might complain about rap, EDM or other genre-heavy channel. I love rap, EDM and other music, but I like making money more. Hence, I usually put Spotify on something nondescript.

- Waze or Google Maps? – I live by Google Maps, because it contains a lane assist. I don't know what bossy bottom decided the layout of the lanes in the Bay Area, but driving there is a constant labor of being forced out of the lane you are driving in or being forced to turn. I found that if you accidentally took passengers over the Golden Gate Bridge to San Rafael when they really just wanted to go to the Marina, you generally didn't get a very high star rating.

  If you live in a less lane crazy place try Waze. However, Waze lacks lane assist, and anticipating what lane you need to be in not just now, but two turns down, is paramount in maintaining your shiny star rating. Waze's vivid colors make the navigation easier, but I don't use Waze because I feel it could be dangerous. It displays ads as you drive near certain destinations, and it is distracting. The last thing I need is an advertisement for McNuggets flashing in my face as I cruise at top speed down the highway in heavy traffic. No Waze no! Bad Waze! Bad McNuggets.

- Puke pack – If someone starts blowing chunks in your car, I recommend you video record them or save any video from your dash cam. You can receive money if someone hurls in your car for cleaning, but of course the passenger is free to dispute your claim. At the very least, you will need to submit pictures of the vom to back up your story.

If you drive at night, I recommend having a "puke pack" in your trunk including such things as paper towels, anti-bacterial wipes, and some sort of cleaning product for when this nightmare happens.

Highway to the Danger Zone

The media loves stories about crime committed by Uber drivers. Journalists practically jizz themselves whenever something comes up about drivers who abuse their passengers and vice-versa. Except for when I almost died when a drunk driver hit my car, I generally felt pretty safe as an Uber driver.

"Aren't you scared to be doing this?" a female passenger from Berkeley said to me once. "I could literally stab you in the neck, since you are driving and not paying attention to me."

I felt mildly scared that night. But not as much as the time a passenger said he had been in jail for attempted murder. Then he said he was kidding, and doctors had diagnosed him as a "chronic nymphomaniac"—this made me feel a lot better.

As a driver, I think it would be a good idea to install a dash cam and even carry mace, but when you think of the millions of rides that happen daily across the world, I am surprised there aren't in fact more altercations between Uber passengers and drivers.

If you find yourself wondering, "Is it safe?" here are some things that can make you worry less. There is some accountability with the star-rating for both drivers and passengers. Uber boots drivers who drop below a certain threshold off the platform, while drivers can avoid picking up passengers with bad ratings. The GPS in the app follows everywhere that you go, so there is a measure of safety that comes with that. Also, all the drivers have had background checks, so felons and people with recent DUI convictions have been weeded out.

There were times I did feel unsafe as a driver though. Uber's GPS is notoriously unreliable, and would often send me behind the place the passenger had requested. One night while a woman waited for me to pick her up, the GPS sent me meandering back into a sketchy San Jose trailer park. The trailer park was called Victory Court, and I remember thinking that none of the people there looked all that victorious.

One problem that came from driving at night was aggressive drunk people. I most felt unsafe on a Lyft ride in which a two male friends and a girl were riding home from a burrito place after partying all night. One man kept beating on his overweight friend and calling him a "pussy ass n***a" to impress his girl. He would punch his friend, who was seated next to me in shotgun, and he kept saying he was a "pussy ass motherfucker." I just grit my teeth and sped down the highway, because his house was close. After dropping them off, he started punching his heavy friend in the street. I peeled out, then pulled over and reported the incident to Lyft via the app. I got an automated response from Lyft saying they would investigate the situation. However, as the driver they never tell you how they end up handling it.

The Petty Olympics

The ability to rate passengers anonymously after driving them somewhere led to great joy on my part. It allows drivers to strike back at unpleasant people.

I never really worried about my star rating, since it was pretty easy to keep a high driver rating — bribing passengers with Twix made me a 5 Star diva. I was pretty much set. If one person happened to rate you poorly, you would easily be able to balance out the stars with other rides. If you drop below 4.7 stars you should worry, though, since conventional wisdom says that is when you are in danger of being booted from the platform as a driver. A Google search on the subject points to articles that suggest 4.6 stars is the GPA for failure as an Uber driver. However, I am not privy to how they decide to get rid of drivers, so I can't say this is the Uber Gospel.

Low ratings for passengers are a huge red flag. To get a good rating as a passenger, you just have to be a decent person and sit there. Sadly, this is too much to ask for some people. If you are riding with Uber, keep in mind that this is not *Driving Miss Daisy*. Rideshare drivers are not your transportation peasants. You are riding in the driver's property, and at the end of the ride the Uber drivers will be rating you.

I think it is important to note I am a smart ass. Snark is part of my genetic code, and I have never been one to take being insulted lightly. If someone says something rude to me, I will clap back and reduce you to tears. It was extremely difficult for me bite my lip every time people were rude to me, as it happened all the time. So I focused on anger management to avoid losing my cool in front of the "pax-holes"—driver slang for asshole passengers. You are normally only going to be spending twelve minutes or so with any rider, so it is never worth it to let some jerk get to you. I taped a picture of Bahia Beach in Brazil on my steering wheel, since that is where I wanted to go with the money I made from Uber. When someone pissed me off, I would touch the picture, and think about how nice the beach will be when I get there and am free from rideshare passengers for the rest of my life.

I consider this chapter the Petty Olympics. Being petty and napping are two of my finest talents, so if they were events in the Olympics I would surely take bronze. Or maybe even silver.

I doubt I'll ever see these fuckwads ever again. I am going to say exactly what I wanted to say to these jerks in this chapter, while teaching you Uber passenger etiquette.

Some explanation as to the rating system is needed. After each ride the passengers can rate the drivers 1 – 5 stars. The drivers also rate the passengers 1 – 5 stars. There are various gambits I used as a driver to keep my rating high. It would really be useful if Uber and Lyft provided an "engagement meter," because you have to decide soon after a person enters your car whether they want to talk or not. Sometimes people just want to zone out and fiddle about on Instagram in the back seat, whereas some people will want to talk. It would be useful if passengers could indicate their preference when they are requesting a ride, but the app doesn't. You must rely on body language and other visual cues as to how social your passenger is feeling.

I loved being petty and dishing out one star ratings to paxholes. Giving one stars to people gave me a warm fuzzy. First of all, there are the annoying bitches that don't take into account tech glitches. If you are a passenger, you need to keep in mind usually the driver is doing their best to get to you safely. The GPS might accidentally send the driver to a side street or somewhere near your request.

For the most part, the star rating I doled out to passengers was in direct proportion to their sarcasm and snarkiness. One time the GPS sent me to the side street of a woman I needed to pick up, and upon her entering my car said in a nasty tone, "Is there a reason you didn't pick me up on Phelan Street?" Because the GPS sent me to another street, you bitch. She hunched over her cell phone not speaking for the entirety of her twenty minute ride—blonde hair cascading over her rose gold iPhone 7. So not only was she rude to me, she went out of her way to avoid engaging with me. Guess what, cunt? One star for you. I'm not your boyfriend. I'm a stranger providing a service to you.

Sarcasm in general will get you one star. Like if you have a temperature request or wish the volume to be turned up or down, don't forget what your Grandmamma told you. Just say "please." I picked up one tech douche in SoMa (South of Market) San Francisco during rush hour. When he hopped in my car, he asked for the air conditioner. His thick framed glasses set off his enticing man bun. I turned on the air conditioner, but the car wasn't cold enough for him. Instead of nicely asking me to lower the temperature he said in a stanky manner, "Is that thing (the air conditioner) working?" One star for you, you dickless, cum-bubble.

Then there are the passengers that think they are smarter than Google Maps. If you know a more efficient route than is displayed on Google Maps, you can suggest a route in a polite manner. Let's be honest, by and large people know the fastest route to their homes from their work or the airport or wherever. Google Maps is not someone's opinion. It is simply a mathematical algorithm. If you know a better route speak the Hell up before Siri (that unreliable bitch) tells me to go on an exit you know is slower.

I picked up one breeder and his annoying family from SFO, and drove his extremely noisy and stupid children home in the rain. He kept needling me with suggestions and criticism of my driving. "You should have exited back there." "Jesus, why are you going this way?" "You better get that thing checked out" he snorted pointing at my smart phone. You know what you better get checked out, buddy? Your tiny pencil dick and gaping asshole. The wife was so embarrassed by her husband's rudeness she gave me a large cash tip, but I still gave these shit biscuits one star.

One way to guarantee you get one star from drivers is to request Uber Pool or Lyft Line (the carpool feature), and harass the driver when he goes to pick up another customer. That is why Uber Pool is cheaper, assholes. That is why you are paying $9 instead of $16 (or whatever). It is because we are picking up other people going in the same direction. So if passengers were like, "Oh my, where are we going?" when they had used the Uber Pool feature, I baptized them with one star.

Though the advent of in-app tipping has eliminated the need for this to some extent, people who didn't tip on a trip to the airport only received one star from me. I would rather have an enema from pure Louisiana Tabasco than drive to SFO airport on a busy night. Most drivers probably feel the same, even though I am sure there are some sick fucks who want Tabasco up the butt. So please tip for these rides.

I christened passengers who had racist or homophobic conversations with one star. My personal pet peeve is when people use the word "gay" as a pejorative. "Gay" is not synonymous with the word "bad." Even though many imagine San Francisco as a gay capital, people there can be just as homophobic and shitty as the rest of the country—especially as SF's status as a gay destination wanes. There is an exodus of LGBTQs out (to more affordable places) while money-hungry, tech bro, douche nuggets stream into the Bay Area at an alarming rate.

I remember one fashionable Asian female passenger was riding with me. I liked her until she talked about how "gay" the event she was going to was. She wasn't going to a gay bar or something. She wasn't going to a screening of *Paris is Burning* at the Castro Theater. I was her Uber driver, so I knew exactly where she was going. She was clearly using the word to mean "sucks" or "shitty." I have a special hate in my heart for homophobic, cisgender women. 1. You are a marginalized group as well. 2. You fall over yourselves to get clothing from LGBTQ fashion designers, hair styling from gay stylists and makeup done by flaming makeup artists. What makes me hate these people in particular is that instead of seeing us as humans, when we aren't propping them up as fashionable accessories to make them look better, they have the temerity to use our descriptor as a put down. So that event you are going to might be "gay," but you know what else is gay? Your driver, you dumb cunt. Waiter. Oh, waiter. Would you please give this clueless heffa a piping hot bowl of one star soup?

There are lots of other one star-worthy actions. Drivers will deduct stars if you make them wait or eat in a vehicle. Also, if you have a clearly audible conversation on the phone for the entirety of the ride, then you are at risk of getting your dose of one star Oxycontin.

Ordinarily, touching the picture of the beach in Brazil kept my cool. But one time, I lost it and just don't give a fuck. A scrawny guy and his aunts got in my car drunk in the middle of the day. They were having a laugh, and it was the guy's birthday. Then the guy who was seated next to me said, "You know who you look like? Zach Galifianakis."

Zach is a funny actor. He was great in *The Hangover*. But I don't believe there is anywhere in God's great universe that being told you look like Zach Galifianakis is a compliment. So I decided to dish back. "Do you know who you look like? Gollum from *Lord of the Rings*. Did you find the Precious?"

Sméagol shut the fuck up real fast after that. He wasn't happy I said this. I think I got one star from him, but I'm sorry—you need to check your edges before you come for me. I will snatch your weave and leave you bald as Sasha Velour on a two dollar Tuesday. Happy birthday!

One way to avoid the star debacle altogether is to ditch passengers. Full disclosure: doing this might get you fired, especially if you do it too often. But, there are people you just shouldn't deal with, especially if they sound falling-down drunk or irritated before your ride has even started. If people are requesting an Uber and are clearly trying to shove their friend who is too inebriated to stand into your car, I suggest ditching them. Hand them a bottle of Crystal Geyser and let them sober up. If you let them in, they might puke in your car. There are other liability issues with sloppy drunks as well. As a rule, I felt it was worth taking a possible hit to my acceptance rating, than to deal with someone who didn't know which way was up.

Also, you should ditch people who are rude before they even enter the car. One time I stopped in downtown San Jose to pick up a young man in his twenties. I followed the GPS and stopped where it indicated on the map. I didn't see anyone, so I called and the passenger said in a snotty manner, "You were supposed to pick me up on the other side of the street."

This is my car. I am not "supposed" to do anything. But you know what you are supposed to do, motherfucker? You are supposed to lick my chode and fondle my balls. I ditched him and drove off as he yelled, "Wait! Wait!" behind me. Damn, it felt good to take gold in the Petty Olympics that day.

One in the Pink

In early 2017, a video of Uber CEO Travis Kalanick surfaced in which he berated an Uber driver. Apparently the driver leased an expensive vehicle to drive for Uber's high-end services. But Uber greedily gobbled up more of the money paid to drivers and put this guy in the red.

The video shows a tipsy-looking Kalanick in the back seat with a couple babes. You see Travis doing some cringeworthy backrolls to a song by the Weeknd. After the driver confronts Travis about Uber's fares, Kalanick yells at the man, "Some people don't take responsibility for their own shit!" The driver had a dash cam with audio, and the video of this incident went viral.

The ensuing embarrassment meant that Uber's PR flacks needed to fart out an apology that Kalanick, "must fundamentally change as a leader and grow up." Well guess what Travis? You are 41 years old, motherfucker. Your ass is grown. Uber subsequently ousted Travis Kalanick as CEO. With his $6.3 billion fortune to frolic about in like Scrooge McDuck in the Money Bin, I shan't be weeping for his misfortunes any time soon.

The saga of Kalanick is just another brick in the story of Uber as an evil empire. From accusations of sexual harassment in the office to the way the corporation disrupted the transportation industry by stomping out taxi companies from city to city—the company can't shake their ruthless image. I wouldn't go back to the way things were before rideshare existed, but I have trouble trusting them.

Hence why many drivers feel drawn to Lyft as the alternative. As a Yin to Uber's Yang, Lyft sells itself as a company that puts compassion over ambition. I would compare Uber vs. Lyft to a Coke vs. Pepsi-like rivalry. At this stage in the game it is more like Coke vs. RC Cola. Or Coke vs. Grape Fanta. I was eager to drive for Lyft, because I noticed that they advertised on gay-friendly media such as the podcast *Rupaul: What's the Tee? with Michelle Visage.* LGBTQs tend to be famously loyal to companies that support our community, so I filed Lyft in my brain somewhere between Absolut and Subaru. Also, the conventional wisdom among Uber drivers was that

Lyft—with its adorable pink mustache logo—had customers that were cuter and nicer than on Uber. I believe it bears mentioning that Lyft has incorporated in-app tips for years while Uber drivers nearly had to riot in the streets to get the same thing. It was basically fucking Dunkirk to get some tips at Uber.

Unfortunately as of 2017, Lyft does not have the brand penetration of Uber. To make money via Lyft I had to stay in San Francisco city to make it worth my while. Whereas, even in the suburbs Uber would be busy all the time. As an example of how cutthroat Uber as a company is, I had many, many more passengers cancel on me via Lyft, which I suspect were cancellations by Uber employees to discourage the Lyft drivers.

Also, several times Uber "brand ambassadors" would get in my car after requesting me via Lyft in order to convince me to drive for Uber—since the law considers drivers private contractors rather than employees at this point, I was free to drive for both companies. And Uber was free to have representatives ride Lyft to poach their drivers.

Ultimately, I would not have been able to sustain a living via Lyft, but I did incorporate it into my weekly strategy. For example, I would attempt to drive the Uber target for the week (which could be anywhere from twenty-five to seventy rides), but if Uber was slow or I didn't feel like dealing with rude Uber pax-holes that day, I would switch on Lyft. It is worth noting that Uber doesn't have the monopoly on pax-holes. Some Lyft users are there because their passenger rating was so low they had been excommunicated from Uber. These passengers still needed to get around hence their need to ride the Pink Moustache.

In terms of branding, I do think Uber has the better position at this moment. Uber became the noun and verb for "rideshare" amongst the populace—like when people say "Kleenex" to mean "tissue" or "iPad" to mean "tablet device." Sometimes passengers would request me via Lyft, and when I arrived they would ask, "Are you my Uber?"

Personally, I prefer Lyft, but in the end if I need a ride I'll usually look at both of them and select the one that is cheaper. Lyft reciprocated my love for them by finally sending me the "Lyft amp" after completing several hundred rides. This is a special light that drivers put in their front window. The amp sparkles rainbow unicorn colors for people to find their rides at night. When the amp is turned off, it sort of looks like a large black dildo from behind. Maybe Lyft founders Logan Green and John Zimmer are using it on each other? What's the Tee, indeed!

By the Numbers

My rideshare career included more than 2000 Uber rides and 500 Lyft rides. I'd love to write a full breakdown, but sometimes you just need the author to shut up and show you a pretty infographic.

UBER DIVA

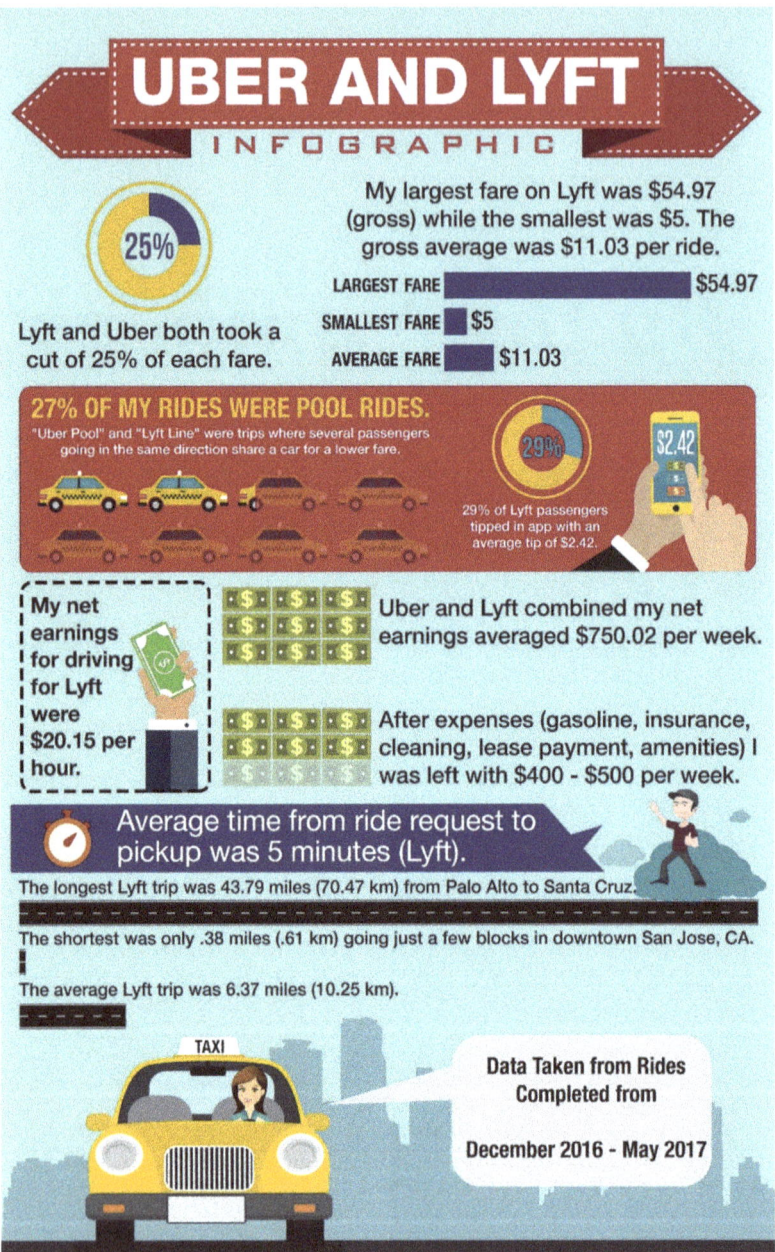

The diva's strategy for getting her hustle on included mostly working at night. Though I drove at all times of the day depending on my energy level, I felt more comfortable driving at night as people were more relaxed and the traffic was less intense. Anyone who has been to the Bay Area knows that the highways of San Francisco can be like your Aunt Edna when she hasn't eaten her prunes: constipated and anger-inducing.

Since I lived in Silicon Valley, about 90% of my trips originated there, but if I wanted to rack up more rides toward a goal, I'd cruise an hour north to San Francisco to tool about the Mission and the Castro. Time of day definitely affected who was riding. After 9:00 p.m. people will have had a drink and be in a good mood. Then with bars closing at 2:00 a.m., from 1:00 a.m. to 3:00 a.m. you have what I call "clean up time" when people filter out of clubs and bars and go home.

From 3:00 a.m. to 6:00 a.m. the world begins to wake up and you get lucrative rides to the local airports or girls going to work at Starbucks (college students who work at Starbucks often don't have money for cars and will commute via Uber). In addition to Starbucks employees, people going to work at other establishments that open and close after public transit ends will commute via Uber. This will open up a new income avenue for Lyft and Uber should they choose to target these consumers more aggressively. So on the late end, we got bartenders and strippers who went home after closing. On the opposite end, the early morning employees going to Starbucks, grocery stores and bagel shops might take us prior to the morning rush.

Sideshow Freaks

OK, this is the chapter you have been waiting for. I know it. You have been wanting to ask me about the wildest Uber passengers. Yes, even crazier than the ones I listed in the "Petty Olympics" chapter. Step right up! Step right up! Meet the people who scared me, baffled me and gave me enough cocktail party conversation to last for the next couple years. Here are the wild ones, the weirdos and the freaks you have been waiting for.

1. Behold! The people who offer drivers drugs while they are driving.

Back when I drove a taxi, a passenger gave me a capsule of Molly. I stashed that pill in an empty Altoids can for months, and frankly I was scared. Do I really want to take drugs from strangers? What if it were cut with some type of poison? However, I remembered I picked them up from a trendy lesbian night in San Francisco, so I inferred it wasn't going to kill me. In the name of guerilla journalism, dear reader, I did that Molly for you. I don't endorse narcotics in any way. Drugs are bad, kids. "Just say no!" But this was MDMA from trendy lesbians, so I didn't really have a choice. I deserve a Purple Heart or sainthood for that. It was a nice roll, but it ended after only about 45 minutes. I think the capsule was stepped on with Advil or baking soda.

During my term as an Uber driver, I noticed this trend was common, but rather than Molly it was coke. About once a month strangers offered me cocaine while I was driving.

One night I took a group of Filipino hetero guys to an after-hours event in downtown San Francisco and a bro kept trying to shove his key in my nose. "Come on, guy.

Just a bump! Have a bump! You're the best Uber driver ever! Come on have a bump!"

I have somehow made it to my forties without ever getting a DUI. I have fucked up a lot of things in my life, but I will never make this mistake. I'm too dainty for prison life. I don't need some shadowy rapist named Bubba licking his chops at me and beckoning, "New FISH! Just my WISH!" So I politely declined his kind offer of a solid rail of Escobar's finest, but I truly appreciated the sentiment.

Another ride, it was a weeknight witching hour in Silicon Valley, and I pulled into an industrial-looking parking lot where a large cargo truck had stopped. An extremely attractive Latino guy stepped out from behind the cargo truck and got in shot gun carrying several bottles of alcohol in a plastic bag. He had broad shoulders and smelled like Gaultier's Le Male. In the transparent plastic bag he carried with the booze it also revealed ... is that? Is that what I think it is? I felt fairly certain the transparent bag also held a few dozen tiny Ziploc baggies of coke. I'm not sure whether this was for sale or personal use, but the guy was clearly where the party was at. Woman after woman called him during the ride, and he gave me the run down on each of his possible paramours for the night. He then took a little baggy out and rubbed it on my nose. He slapped the baggy teasingly back and forth across my nose five or six times while I cruised at top speed down Highway 101.

"You want this don't you? Gotta have it, huh?"

"Well, not at this particular moment."

When I dropped him off, he offered me a bump which I declined. Do I look like someone who wants a "dance with Belinda" (my euphemism for cocaine) before he drives? Clearly, people think this diva wants to drive around all the time jacked up on disco dust. But alas, I would never drive while high or drunk. That's what Uber is for. Anyway, he gave me a solid cash tip as he hopped out to meet his lady friends for a night of festivities.

2. Behold! The man who was left at the trap house

Driving through a desolate area of San Jose at night, I received a ping to pick up a hippie woman from an In-N-Out Burger. The fast food establishment was closed for the evening, and I sat there waiting and eventually called the number. Instead of a female hippie, I was surprised when an African-American guy hopped in my car. He said that the woman had requested him the ride, and then the woman confirmed via text she had.

The man told me he had gone out with his friends and they abandoned him at a "trap house"—a run-down house in the hood used for cooking or smoking crack. I wasn't directly in front of the house, but there were a few guys loitering about the In-N-Out parking lot that were missing teeth, so I imagined it must be close by. His friends had gone off to go smoke crack, and he felt dejected by this betrayal. Much like Dear Abby, I am famous for dispensing pearls of wisdom. I told the guy, "If your friends are going to ditch you at a crack house, I don't think they are very good friends."

"But these guys and I, we go way back. We cool and all."

"That's fine and dandy, but if a rocky form of the popular stimulant is going to be more important to them than you, it is clearly in your best interests to delete them from your Snapchat."

    3. Behold! The drunk man dressed as a Ninja Turtle!

I basically made my rent driving the hour before the bars close and the hour after. During clean up time, you have a good couple hours to make that coin before the city sleeps for the night.

Of course, this is also the time that is most dangerous for violent drunks and plain old fucked up people. One thing that drunk people often do is they request a ride, and then walk away from the point from which they have a requested the ride.

After last call in San Jose, I drove to pick someone up. He wasn't at the GPS location, so I called and he spoke frantically trying to describe where he was. He walked a good half mile away from the request point, but when I finally found him, I saw that he was dressed as a Ninja Turtle. This guy was really cute, and I felt a little turned on by the way his chest filled out the Michelangelo costume. I think he noticed my admiration and quipped, "Are those some nunchucks in your pocket or are you just happy to see me?"

The ping had said he wanted a ride back all the way to Oakland, but he told me he had his car in San Jose. Clearly in no condition to drive home, I gave sparky some bottled water and left him near Denny's so he could get some coffee and sober up.

4. Behold! The Persian stripper with her titty out!

Monday nights in the Castro are popular with college kids both gay and straight, because they have $1 wells at a few bars. During clean up time this Monday night, a few drunkards ambled across the street. I'm looking for "Niyousha" who had requested me via Lyft. I find her outside of Q Bar. A couple of her friends are vomiting onto the side walk. *Oh, shit. Cancel the ride. Cancel the ride.* I panic as Niyousha forces open the door dropping the contents of her burrito onto my back seat.

"Are you our Uber?" she burped spilling corn out of the burrito down on the floor mat. One of her breasts flopped out of her sparkly halter top, and her friend covered her with a jacket. They start piling into the car just as I finally got the app to cancel the ride. "Is that 'Bad and Boujee' on the radio? Turn this up. It's my jam." Niyousha planted her ass firmly in my back seat.

"You and your friends are too drunk. Here's some water. I had to cancel the ride."

"No you're fucking not. I gotta get to Crazy Horse. I gotta make bank." By this time half the burrito is in the bottom of my car.

"They are vomiting. I can't let them in here. And now you are getting sour cream on the upholstery. This ride is over. I'm sorry I can't help you."

"You're fucking driving me. You're my Uber!"

It's getting ugly, so I turn on the video camera of my phone in case an incident happened.

"I'm kindly asking you to get out."

"Well we're reporting you then."

Her tall friend who looked like the typical entitled snowflake starts typing in the phone, "I'm reporting you for assholeness. Correct. Bitch. Yes. Piece of shit. Probably so."

It didn't even make any sense, but that's what he said in the video.

"Can't even drive to pick us up." Niyousha adds. Even though I had already picked them up.

Their one friend who had finally stopped vomiting hastened their departure, "Get out. Get out. Get out."

"Bye Felicia!" I say as they get out.

Tell Me Sweet Little Lies

Did your parents raise you to believe lying is wrong? I know Latinos get slapped by *la chancla* if *abuela* catches you in a fib.

Would you believe me if I told you your granny was full of shit? Lying is useful. Lying is fun. Lying also gives me a warm fuzzy. As a rideshare driver you need to perfect the true art of the little white lie.

So hear me out. I do not endorse lying to your partner or your *abuela*. Keep it 100 if you are before a judge in a court of law. But to that rube you are taking to the airport at 5AM—go right ahead. Fib all you want. In the entire 6 months and thousands of Uber and Lyft rides I gave, I only had the same passenger once.

First of all, you should lie to avoid topics that make you uncomfortable. One of my personal philosophies is "you can't blame people for the most obvious response." Like if you are pregnant, people will ask how far along you are. Or if you are from West Virginia, older people will make a John Denver reference when they meet you.

For me, I wish to avoid talking about my hometown. I grew up in Kansas City, but haven't lived there full-time in more than twenty years. To avoid that conversation when passengers asked, "Are you from here?" I just learned to zip my lip and say, "Yup." Because honesty, in this case, means half an hour of talking about local sports teams I know nothing about and whether my family voted Republican.

In addition, I think you should lie about WARPS: War Religion Politics and Sex. The subjects that will invariably get you in trouble. You can be right or you can be liked, but you probably can't be both. Think of the conversation with passengers like a conversation at Thanksgiving before your cousin gets drunk and starts talking about the FEMA camps—keep it nonchalant or just agree with whatever the passenger says. Then you will see your star rating rise sky high.

I also used lying as a gambit to open conversations. This is because of my Indian passengers. I noticed I had trouble connecting with the many Indians of Silicon Valley. The riders would bring spicy food in the car, and they would talk amongst themselves in their local languages such as Hindi or Punjabi. They made me feel like a failure as a driver, since I imagined they liked the

US enough to come here, but I couldn't get a word in. I wanted to get to know them and learn a little about India.

I imagined they were tired of white people asking them about Indian restaurants, so I thought about how everyone loves to brag about wherever they are from. I started lying and saying, "You know my friend is getting married in India next year, and I'm going for the first time. Where should I check out?" This turned out to be a good move, since then I would have a lively conversation with the person for the duration of the ride. And I learned about the Ayurveda healing centers in Kerala, party beaches of Goa and the mystic valleys of the Himalayas.

The "lie about a wedding" strategy turned out great, since the rider will think you are very invested in going and will go to great lengths to tell you about their home. It doesn't have to be foreigners though. If I met people from the US whose regions have a reputation as being "Podunk" or "Yocal," they often loved telling me all about it more than anything. So if I met someone from say South Carolina or Nebraska (I'm from Kansas City, I know your pain), then I would just say, "My roommate from college is getting married there next year, and I'm in the wedding. Where should I check out?" Awkward silence solved!

So while you are driving for Uber, think of the truth as the age listed on a profile for a dating app like Tinder or Scruff: what is listed is merely a suggestion. So I'll reiterate. In life, honesty is the best policy. But for twelve minutes on a Friday night with someone you have nothing in common? It is obviously a great way to avoid topics you hate and break the ice. Go ahead and fib to your heart's content.

Glitch Nation

As a driver, one thing you must learn to live with is glitches. When I was a contractor in Silicon Valley, I learned that even these amazing tech bastions have their share of glitches. Engineers at any big tech firm love to create innovative new programs. Then these programs get buggy and no one bothers with maintenance. I'm not saying this happened on the projects I worked, but bugs and glitches are a part of life in the tech world.

That means that the driver apps for Lyft and Uber have plenty o' glitches. Lyft's driver app could be particularly frustrating as I would have to press a special button to say the passenger was in my car, and sometimes the app would not acknowledge this. It felt dangerous, since I was driving around trying to get the app to realize I had the person in my car. Until the app recognizes a person is in your car, their destination will not appear in the app so

I'm just driving around like a mad fool as the passengers get more and more irritated.

Uber's app could be even more infuriating, because sometimes it would accept a passenger and wouldn't tell me. Then ten minutes later I received the message that so-and-so had canceled his ride. And I would be like, *I haven't even accepted this guy!*

As stated earlier, I found Google Maps to be the sturdier app in the turn-by-turn navigation department. Google Maps did have one major glitch: highway overpasses. Sometimes when going on an overpass or in a cloverleaf, Google Maps would get confused and start to suggest that I take the wrong exit. I ruined one Indian gentleman's ride, because I didn't realize this at first and went around all four sections of a cloverleaf in Silicon Valley. I don't think I got five stars for that ride.

Probably the worst glitch appearance happened when Uber Pool wanted me to pick up several people from La Vic Taqueria in San Jose. The Uber app didn't tell me to pick up the second person there until I had driven ten minutes toward the first guy's destination. I then had to make the choice: A. take the first exit and go back or B. ditch the second passenger and keep driving. I went back to La Vic to get the second passenger, but the first passenger got so upset he wrote to Uber. Then they deducted a portion of my pay for the ride when it was their app that was glitching.

Rode Hard and Put Away Wet

If you think you can drive safely and make a few bucks, go ahead and try Uber and Lyft. I think rideshare is great as a side business, but this work can be challenging to do full-time. Also, it's all fun and games while things are good, but the more you drive the more likely you will at some point be involved in an accident. My back still aches after I exercise and during rains to remind me of my rideshare misadventure. Uber away at your own risk!

This book will soon be a historical document of a short-lived time in transportation history. Much like the Pony Express revolutionized post mail for two years, then disappeared when trains made the ponies useless, Uber and Lyft as we know now are already on their way out.

Sometimes in Mountain View I'd spot Google's self-driving "Waymo" zipping about. GM, Toyota and even Samsung have jumped into the field as well. Uber will need to evolve or perish, since other companies will offer a cheaper driverless version of the same service in the near future. People will go with whatever is most economical—if another company provides a comparable service to Uber at a cheaper rate, consumers will flock to that company.

We don't need to worry about humans being replaced by these services any time soon. My theory is that a human attendant will legally be required in self-driving cars for the foreseeable future. They will take over when glitches inevitably occur, and make sure kids don't vandalize all the vehicles. Riders will treat these vehicles like the floor on Dodgers Stadium and just leave stuff everywhere. This should open up new business opportunities, though. You might be able to franchise fleets of self-driving cars while providing cleaning and maintenance services.

As the "ride experience" becomes paramount to get from point A to point B, entirely new industries might take root. You could have driverless car attendants that are amateur comedians or DJs. Karaoke is already a feature in some Ubers, but in the driverless era, it will be a full-on disco. And aspiring models might get their start as being in-demand attendants. Who wouldn't want to start a night of partying with a hot babe or beefy hunk guiding your self-driving car to your night out? There will need to be watchdog groups, though, as I could see these services easily becoming "brothels on wheels." Having an experienced cartender might beget a whole new profession. Or you could play a "car roulette" and let the car decide where you go out for the evening.

Then there will be car attendants for more practical times, such as licensed child-care professionals to take your kids to school. Have your kids learn the multiplication tables or Spanish while their accredited car tutor escorts them! Car attendants with medical skills can transport the disabled and other special needs situations. Teachers, nurses, singers, DJs, entrepreneurs, comedians: the transportation revolution is happening before us, and we are only limited by our imaginations!

Random Ass Things I Laughed About to Keep Myself Entertained While Driving

I get bored easily whilst driving, so I often make fun of location names to amuse myself. For your entertainment, here are the location and business names I made fun of while driving for Uber.

Milpitas City in Silicon Valley – obviously should be "Milpenis."

Burlingame – this boujee suburb is "Burling-lame."

Sunnyvale – My last home in the Bay Area was "Funny-vale" or "Sunny-fail."

San Jose – Hoser.

Superette – Corner grocer in the Haight district of San Francisco was clearly "Smurfette."

Trade Zone (a street in San Jose) – "Trade" means "hot guy" in gay slang. I didn't need to change this location name, I just laughed when I drove past.

Vallejo – Waterfront city in Solano County, clearly meant to be "Valley Ho."

Menlo Park – Venture capital impresarios love to smell the wind in "Menlo Fart."

Portola – Crapola.

Old Ironsides (a street in Santa Clara) – every time I drove past this, I thought of the quote from *Valley of the Dolls*, "He's protecting Old Ironsides." You would have to like old camp movies to think this is amusing.

Squat and Gobble (restaurant) – Cop a squat and gobble.

Panteira (restaurant) – Panty Raid.

Fin.

My Acknowledgements

Special thanks to everyone who showed support to me after my accident, especially my parents! I also want to thank those who contributed to my GoFundMe page "T-Boned by a Drunk Driver" or just took care of me and helped me out. Much like Beyoncé I value the element of surprise, so I didn't reach out to anyone before I initially unveiled this book. I will go ahead and thank Mr. Palo Alto, Kermygirl and Authors Large and Small. Also, I send my heartfelt gratitude to Christopher Wilson, Risunotabi, Adrock, Ben and William Hamilton, Marcella Hammer, Bearded_NASJ, Sharkey, Judy, Danika Okano, Cydonie, Danae Winters, Leia, Rosie Luscious, Lady Luna, Kalani and several friends and contributors who wish to remain anonymous.

Here's a shout out to Elizabeth Shoemaker. You've been a hot, sassy and fabulous friend of over 20 years.

Also, I'd like to thank my attorneys at Tran & Associates. Danny and Edwin, you are the best. Much love to the staff at El Camino Hospital. Big hugs to my chiropractors—especially Dr. Jeff Remsburg at Active Health Solutions in Prairie Village, KS. They helped me realign and reignite following my accident.

Author's Bio, Book and Websites

Meet Charles St. Anthony

Charles acquired his BA from Columbia University in East Asian Studies with an emphasis on Japanese, and his MA in the same subject from Sophia University in Tokyo, Japan. He subsequently worked as a translator for American celebrities visiting Japan, appeared on Japanese TV as a foreign commentator, and even appeared in a Japanese movie called *Juoku En Kasegu!* (The Billion Yen Jackpot!).

Other Books

Impossibly Glamorous

This book is an autobiographical account of Charles' travails growing up gay in Kansas then working as a Japanese media personality in Tokyo. Hilarious, heartwarming and full of celebrity dish, check for *Impossibly Glamorous* at your favorite online retailer today!

San Francisco Daddy

Charles' second memoir is a dissertation on love and life as a single gay man in San Francisco. Whether it is his dating fiascoes in the Castro or beating his way down to Silicon Valley, you'll love his adventures in the New Age Babylon by the Bay.

DTLA Hustler

In this mini-masterpiece you explore the food scene of the downtown Los Angeles (DTLA) Renaissance. See how Charles did this while losing weight simultaneously by delivering on foot and bicycle. Packed with photos and cute visuals, this brisk read gives you the down low on how to make money while becoming a "Skinny Sensation." Pick up a copy and get hustling today!

Website

Keep the hustle going by signing up to the mail list at dtlahustler.com.

Social Media

Follow Charles on social media @kingcharles0921 on Instagram or Twitter.

Podcast
T with Charles

Charles St. Anthony takes on the scalding hot topics in current events and entertainment. Charles brings a dash of wit and wisdom to his take on the hard-hitting (or just ridiculous) news stories of our day. Available on all major podcast platforms.

###